# Shaping
## Materials

## Chris Oxlade

Crabtree Publishing Company
www.crabtreebooks.com

# Crabtree Publishing Company

www.crabtreebooks.com

**Editors:** Hayley Leach, Adrianna Morganelli, Michael Hodge
**Senior Design Manager:** Rosamund Saunders
**Designer:** Ben Ruocco
**Photographer:** Philip Wilkins

**Photo credits:** 1Apix/Alamy p. 6, Chris Alack/Getty Images p. 17, Tim Caddick/Alamy p. 23, Darrin Jenkins/Alamy p. 16, Fortune fish/Alamy p. 12, Jeff Morgan/Alamy p. 11, Janine Wiedel Photolibrary /Alamy p. 21, Xela/Alamy p. 15, Ute Kaiser/zefa/Corbis p. 7, Michael Keller/Corbis p. 9, Tom Stewart/Corbis cover and p. 20, Paul Jones/Getty Images p. 13, Jeremy Liebman/Getty Images p. 10, Joel Sartore/National Geographic/Getty Images p. 19, Chris Oxlade p. 14, Richard Jung/Photolibrary.com p. 8, Peter Weimann/Photolibrary.com p. 24, Steve Allen/Science Photo Library p. 18, R. Maisonneuve, Publiphoto Diffusion/Science Photo Library p. 25, Rosenfield Images Ltd/Science Photo Library p. 22, Philip Wilkins pp. 26-27.

**Activity & illustrations:** Shakespeare Squared pp. 28-29.

**Cover:** A potter is using clay to make a pot.

**Title page:** A worker uses a chisel to shape a stone archway.

The publishers would like to thank the models Philippa and Sophie Campbell for appearing in the photographs.

Because of the nature of the Internet, it is possible that some website addresses (URLs) included in this book may have changed, or sites may have changed or closed down since publication. While the author and publisher regret any inconvenience this may cause the readers, no responsibility for any such changes can be accepted by either the author or the publisher.

**Library and Archives Canada Cataloguing in Publication**

Oxlade, Chris
    Shaping materials / Chris Oxlade.

(Working with materials)
Includes index.
ISBN 978-0-7787-3641-7 (bound).--ISBN 978-0-7787-3651-6 (pbk.)

    1. Materials--Juvenile literature. 2. Materials--Experiments--Juvenile
literature. I. Title. II. Series: Oxlade, Chris. Working with materials.

TA403.2.O95 2007    j620.1'1    C2007-904319-4

**Library of Congress Cataloging-in-Publication Data**

Oxlade, Chris.
  Shaping materials / Chris Oxlade.
    p. cm. -- (Working with materials)
  Includes index.
  ISBN-13: 978-0-7787-3641-7 (rlb)
  ISBN-10: 0-7787-3641-5 (rlb)
  ISBN-13: 978-0-7787-3651-6 (pb)
  ISBN-10: 0-7787-3651-2 (pb)
  1. Materials--Juvenile literature. 2. Materials--Experiments--Juvenile
literature. I. Title. II. Series.

  TA403.2.O953 2007
  620.1'1--dc22

                2007027422

## Crabtree Publishing Company

www.crabtreebooks.com    1-800-387-7650

**Published in Canada**
**Crabtree Publishing**
616 Welland Ave.
St. Catharines, Ontario
L2M 5V6

**Published in the United States**
**Crabtree Publishing**
PMB16A
350 Fifth Ave., Suite 3308
New York, NY 10118

**Published by CRABTREE PUBLISHING COMPANY**
Copyright © **2008**

# CONTENTS

Words in **bold** can be found in the glossary on page 30

# Shaping materials

Everything around you is made up of materials. Everyday materials include paper, plastic, metal, and glass. We use these materials to make objects such as tables, chairs, shoes, cars, and aircraft.

↓ *All of these objects are plastic. They were made by putting liquid plastic into **molds**.*

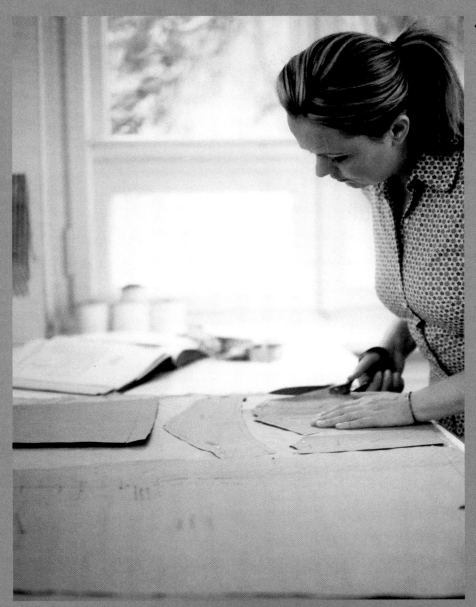

← *A dressmaker is cutting a piece of fabric into the shape she wants using a pair of scissors.*

Some materials come in blocks or sheets. Others come as liquids or powders. Cutting, folding, and molding are some ways of shaping materials into objects. The method that we use depends on the **properties** of the material.

# Scissors and saws

Cutting with scissors is a simple way to make shapes from materials such as paper and fabric. A pair of scissors has two sharp blades that slice through the material.

*↓ This cook is cutting pastry shapes. The pastry cutter has a sharp metal blade.*

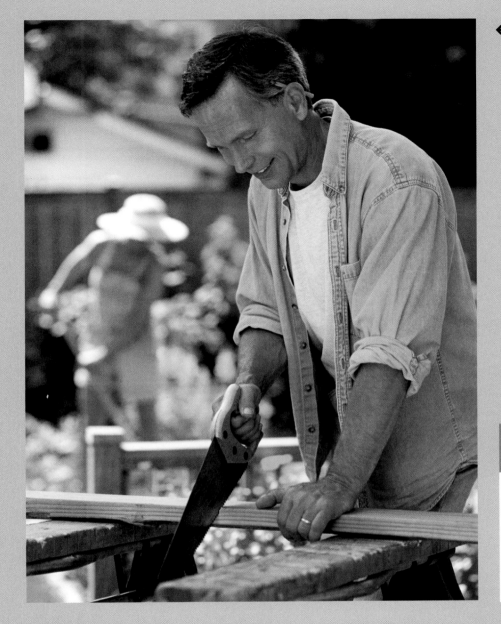

← This **carpenter** is cutting a piece of wood with a saw to make the shape that he wants.

## It's a fact!

When saw blades are made, they are heated and then dipped in water. This makes them extra hard.

We cut through thick pieces of material, such as wood, with a saw. A saw blade has hundreds of sharp grooves called "teeth". As the saw moves backward and forward, the teeth rip away tiny bits of material.

# Carving materials

An artist can make a wooden sculpture by carving a block of wood. The artist cuts bits off of the block using a knife or a sharp tool called a chisel. It takes a lot of skill to cut away the right bits.

↓ *An artist is shaping wood with a chisel.*

↑ *A stone mason chips away stone with a hammer and chisel.*

Artists called stone masons work with stone. They start with a block of stone and gradually chip away pieces to make the shape that they want. We also shape stone blocks to make the walls of buildings.

## It's a fact!

The ancient Egyptians built giant stone pyramids using thousands of stone blocks. Workers cut the blocks using simple hand tools.

# Folding and bending

We can make objects by folding and bending flat sheets of material. For example, we make envelopes and paper bags by folding paper. Cardboard boxes are made by folding stiff cardboard.

*← You can make shapes, such as this flower, by folding a piece of paper.*

↑ *This tent has metal poles. The poles are bent over to make the dome shape of the tent.*

Bending lets us make rounded shapes from flat sheets of materials. For example, shoes are made by bending leather around a wooden block called a "last".

## It's a fact!

A curved wooden chair seat is made by bending flat sheets of wood. The wood is heated with steam to make it easier to bend.

13

# Machine shapers

Many objects are shaped by machines. The machines have blades that cut away material from a block. This leaves the shape that is wanted.

← *This machine cuts wood into shapes. The blade in the middle spins to cut away the wood.*

↑ *A carpenter is making an ornament on a lathe.*

Carpenters and metalworkers often use a machine called a "lathe". It makes round objects, such as rods and poles. The material spins around at a high speed. A blade cuts away the material.

## It's a fact!

Computers control machines to make objects such as nuts and bolts. The computer automatically moves the material and the blades to cut the shape.

15

# Molding materials

Chocolates, ice cubes, and bowls all have something in common. They are all made in a mold. A mold has a **hollow** space inside. The hollow space is the shape of the object being made.

↓ Chocolate is warmed to make it soft. Then it is poured into molds. It gets hard again when it cools.

← Jellies are made by putting a warm jelly mixture into a mold. The jelly turns solid when it cools.

**Runny** material is poured into the mold. It fills the mold to make a new object. The runny material gradually gets hard. Then the object is taken out of the mold. Now the mold is ready to be used again.

# Molding in industry

Nearly all plastic items are made by molding. The plastic is warmed to make it soft. Then it is put into a mold. When the plastic cools, the object is taken out of the mold. Glass objects are also made in molds.

↓ *This plastic can has just been taken out of its mold.*

↑ *This is molten copper. It is being poured into a mold.*

Some metal objects are made in molds. The metal is heated up until it melts. The **molten** metal is poured into a mold. When the metal cools, it turns solid again.

## It's a fact!

Builders use molds to make concrete shapes. They build wooden molds and then pour concrete in. When the concrete is hard, they take away the wood.

# Shaping soft materials

Some materials are easy to shape when they are very soft. Potter's clay is very soft. You can easily shape it with your hands. A potter uses simple tools to shape clay.

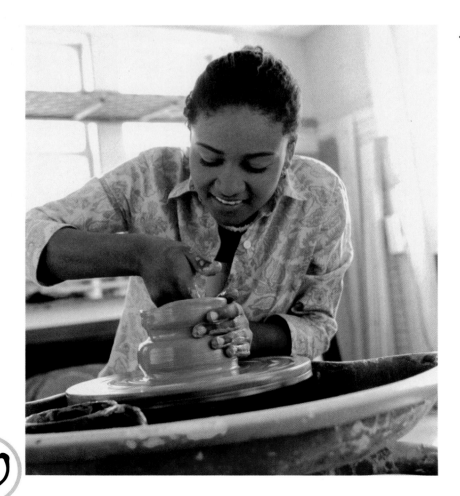

← *This potter is using her hands to shape a clay pot.*

↑ *This glass blower is making a glass vase by blowing air into a blob of hot, soft glass.*

Glass is normally very hard, and it can break easily. Glass gets soft when it is heated. Glass blowers shape glass with special tools when it is hot. Then they let the glass cool and get hard.

## It's a fact!

Soft materials, such as cake icing, can be pushed through a small hole. This makes a long, thin piece of material.

# Shaping metals

Iron, steel, **aluminum**, and copper are all types of metal. They are strong and hard. We shape metals by cutting and molding them.

↓ *This machine is cutting a sheet of metal using a **laser**.*

← *This machine is pressing a metal object into shape.*

## It's a fact!

The round shape of a coin is cut from a sheet of metal. Then another machine presses the picture onto each side of the coin.

We can squash, stretch, bend, and twist a piece of metal. We make objects such as metal bowls and can lids by pressing sheets of metal into shape.

# Hammering and rolling metals

A blacksmith makes items, such as **horseshoes** and garden gates, from iron. The blacksmith heats up the iron. This makes the iron softer and easier for the blacksmith to hammer into shape.

↓ *A blacksmith is making a horseshoe. He is working on a heavy block of iron called an "anvil".*

↑ *Copper is rolled into sheets.*

Thin sheets of metal, such as steel, are made by rollers. The metal starts as a block. The metal is heated to make it easier to roll. It goes through many rollers. It gradually gets thinner and thinner.

## It's a fact!

Metal wire is used to make things like paper clips. Wire is made by stretching a piece of metal a bit at a time. The metal gets thinner and longer.

# See for yourself!

## Molding ice shapes

Create your own molds to make different ice shapes.

| What you need | |
|---|---|
| modeling clay | water |
| plastic food wrap | small object (such as a |
| old saucer | toy building block) |

1. Flatten a large lump of modeling clay until it is about 1 inch (2.5 cm) thick and about 3 inches (8 cm) across.

2. Lay a piece of plastic food wrap loosely over the top of the modeling clay.

3. Press an object firmly into the top of the modeling clay. Now take it off again. You have made a mold of the object.

4. Put the mold on a saucer. Carefully fill the mold with water.

5. Put the saucer in the freezer.

6. When frozen, carefully take the ice out of the mold. You have made a copy of the object out of ice.

# Making a box

Find out how to make a box by cutting and folding.

| **What you need** | |
|---|---|
| pencil | scissors |
| ruler | adhesive tape |
| paper | |

① Copy the pattern here onto a piece
of paper. Cut along the solid lines.
Do not cut along the dotted lines.

② Bend the paper along all of the dotted
lines. Fold all of the side panels up, and
then fold the end tabs around.

③ Using adhesive tape, attach the end tabs
to the side panels. You have made a box.

# Beautiful butterflies

## Making pipe cleaner butterflies

**Fold and bend simple materials into beautiful butterflies!**

**What you need**
colorful construction paper or tissue paper
pencil
colorful pipe cleaners
scissors
ruler

**1.** Choose two pieces of construction paper or tissue paper. Using a ruler, trace a 5-inch (13-cm) square on one sheet and a 4-inch (10-cm) square on the other. Cut out both squares.

**2.** Accordion-fold each square on its diagonal.

**3.** Bend a pipe cleaner in half, creating a small loop on the bottom.

**4.** Pinch the center of each square to form a bow-tie shape. Arrange the squares inside the folded pipe cleaner, with the bow-tie center in the middle. Place the larger square above the smaller one. These are the butterfly's wings.

**5.** Twist the pipe cleaner above and below each pinched square to keep the wings in place.

**6.** Make antennae by curling the top ends of the pipe cleaner.

**What you will see:**
You have now created your own butterfly! You shaped the wings by folding paper, and you shaped the body and antennae by bending and twisting a pipe cleaner. The wire inside the pipe cleaner helped it keep its shape. What other animals can you create from pipe cleaners and paper?

# Glossary

**aluminum** A type of metal that is strong but lightweight

**carpenter** A person who makes things from wood

**horseshoe** A curved piece of iron that gets nailed to a horse's foot

**hollow** An empty space inside a mold

**laser** A device that makes a beam of light

**molten** When something is heated until it melts

**mold** To make an object into a mold

**runny** When something flows like a liquid, such as water

**property** Tells us what a material is like. The hardness of a material and how easily it melts are examples of properties

# Further information

## BOOKS

**How We Use: Metals/Paper/Rubber/Wood**
by Chris Oxlade, Raintree (2005)

**A Material World: It's Glass/It's Metal/It's Plastic/It's Wood**
by Kay Davies and Wendy Oldfield, Wayland (2006)

**Investigating Science: How do we use materials?**
by Jacqui Bailey, Franklin Watts (2005)

## WEBSITES

www.bbc.co.uk/schools/revisewise/science/materials/09_act.shtml
Animated examples and quiz about changing materials

www.strangematterexhibit.com
Fun site about the properties of materials

## PLACES TO VISIT

American Museum of Science and Energy, Tennessee
www.amse.org

The Children's Museum of Science and Technology, New York
www.cmost.com

The Discovery Center for Science and Technology, California
www.discoverycntr.org

# Index

Printed in the USA